MW00584263

Beluga Whales

by Betsy Rathburn

BLASTOFF! READERS
2

BELLWETHER MEDIA • MINNEAPOLIS, MN

Blastoff! Readers are carefully developed by literacy experts to build reading stamina and move students toward fluency by combining standards-based content with developmentally appropriate text.

Level 1 provides the most support through repetition of high-frequency words, light text, predictable sentence patterns, and strong visual support.

Level 2 offers early readers a bit more challenge through varied sentences, increased text load, and text-supportive special features.

Level 3 advances early-fluent readers toward fluency through increased text load, less reliance on photos, advancing concepts, longer sentences, and more complex special features.

★ **Blastoff! Universe**

Reading Level

Grade K

Grades 1–3

Grade 4

This edition first published in 2021 by Bellwether Media, Inc.

No part of this publication may be reproduced in whole or in part without written permission of the publisher. For information regarding permission, write to Bellwether Media, Inc., Attention: Permissions Department, 6012 Blue Circle Drive, Minnetonka, MN 55343.

Library of Congress Cataloging-in-Publication Data

Names: Rathburn, Betsy, author.
Title: Beluga whales / by Betsy Rathburn.
Description: Minneapolis, MN : Bellwether Media, Inc., 2021. | Series: Blast off! readers: animals of the Arctic | Includes bibliographical references and index. | Audience: Ages 5-8 | Audience: Grades K-1 | Summary: "Relevant images match informative text in this introduction to beluga whales. Intended for students in kindergarten through third grade"-- Provided by publisher.
Identifiers: LCCN 2019053740 (print) | LCCN 2019053741 (ebook) | ISBN 9781644872123 (library binding) | ISBN 9781618919700 (ebook)
Subjects: LCSH: White whale--Juvenile literature. | Zoology--Arctic regions--Juvenile literature.
Classification: LCC QL737.C433 R378 2021 (print) | LCC QL737.C433 (ebook) | DDC 599.5/42--dc23
LC record available at https://lccn.loc.gov/2019053740
LC ebook record available at https://lccn.loc.gov/2019053741

Editor: Kieran Downs   Designer: Brittany McIntosh

Printed in the United States of America, North Mankato, MN

Table of Contents

Beluga whales are ocean survivors!

These **mammals** swim through the icy waters of the Arctic **biome**.

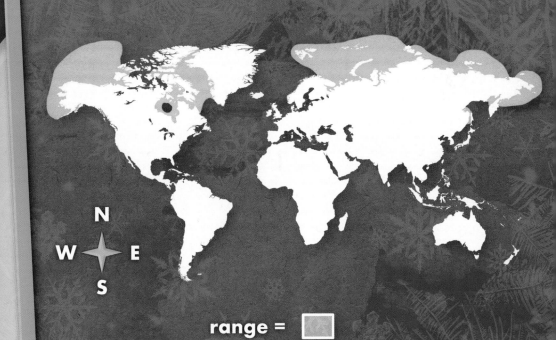

Beluga Whale Range

range =

5

Thick, white sheets of ice
float through Arctic waters.

White skin helps belugas hide among the ice sheets. **Predators** cannot see them!

Belugas have **blubber**. This keeps the whales warm in cold water.

Special Adaptations

hump on back

white skin

thick blubber

The blubber also holds **energy**. It helps belugas survive when they cannot find food!

Belugas lack **dorsal fins**. This helps them move quickly under ice.

They have thick humps on their backs. The humps help belugas break through ice!

Using Their Melons

When belugas dive,
their heartbeats slow.
This helps the whales
hold their breath longer!

blowhole

Belugas go to the surface
for air. They breathe through
their **blowholes**.

Beluga whales use **echolocation**. This helps them travel through Arctic waters.

They wiggle their **melons** to send sounds in different directions!

Beluga Whale Stats

Least Concern	Near Threatened	Vulnerable	Endangered	Critically Endangered	Extinct in the Wild	Extinct

conservation status: least concern

life span: up to 35 years

← melon

Echolocation also helps belugas **communicate**.

Their chirps sound like singing.
Belugas are often called
the canaries of the sea!

Pods and Prey

pod

Beluga whales hunt in shallow waters near coasts. They often hunt in **pods**.

Pods chase down small **prey**. Belugas love to eat fish and crabs!

Beluga Whale Diet

Arctic cod

rose fish

sockeye salmon

Belugas have short teeth.
They cannot tear into prey.
Instead, they swallow their
food whole.

These whales find plenty to eat
in the Arctic biome!

Glossary

biome—a large area with certain plants, animals, and weather

blowholes—holes on the heads of dolphins and whales that let air in and out

blubber—the layer of body fat that helps cold water animals stay warm

communicate—to share thoughts and feelings using sounds, faces, and actions

dorsal fins—fins on the backs of many fish and whales

echolocation—the act of sending out sounds and listening for the echoes to find distant objects

energy—the power to move and do things

mammals—warm-blooded animals that have backbones and feed their young milk

melons—large bumps on beluga whale foreheads that help with echolocation

pods—groups of beluga whales that hunt together

predators—animals that hunt other animals for food

prey—animals that are hunted by other animals for food

To Learn More

AT THE LIBRARY

Johnson, Elizabeth R. *Beluga Whales*. North Mankato, Minn.: Capstone Press, 2017.

Murray, Julie. *Beluga Whales*. Minneapolis, Minn.: Abdo Pub, 2020.

Nugent, Samantha. *Arctic Ocean*. New York, N.Y.: AV2 by Weigl, 2018.

ON THE WEB

FACTSURFER

Factsurfer.com gives you a safe, fun way to find more information.

1. Go to www.factsurfer.com.

2. Enter "beluga whales" into the search box and click 🔍.

3. Select your book cover to see a list of related content.

Index

The images in this book are reproduced through the courtesy of: imageBROKER/ Alamy, front cover, pp. 9, 11, 21; Luna Vandoorne, p. 4; WaterFrame/ Alamy, p. 6; Nature Picture Library/ Alamy, p. 7; Andrea Izzotti, pp. 8, 23; Edward Chin, p. 10; Stock Connection Blue/ Alamy, p. 12; cmeder, p. 13; Wolfgang_Steiner, p. 14; agefotostock/ Alamy, pp. 15, 20; CostinT, p. 16; Miles Away Photography, p. 17; Flip Nicklin/ Age Fotostock, p. 18; Travel Faery, p. 19 (Arctic cod); Vitezslav Halamka, p. 19 (rose fish); Beat J Korner, p. 19 (sockeye salmon).